DEDICATION

To Najat,
a shy 13-year-old girl who had the courage
to overcome her evangephobia for the sake
of the gospel message.

TABLE OF CONTENTS

Intro i

Evangewhat? 1

Facing Down Your Fears 5

Not Cool, Man 9

Get Lost! 13

Say What? 17

Prayer: The Antidote 21

Your Weakness = God's Strength 25

Fueling Your Passion 29

Obedience 101 .33

Love, Love, Love 37

They Need Jesus NOW! 41

Eternity Is a Loooong Time 45

Discovering Your Passion Fuel 49

Religion vs. Relationship 53

BC: Before Christ 57

The Factor: What Opened Your Eyes? 61

After Christ. 65

Dare 2 Share Your Story 69

God Wants to Use You!. 73

Dare 2 Share Jesus' Story 77

GOSPEL Journey[1] 81

GOSPEL Journey[2] 85

Dunamis: Dynamite!. 89

Soul Apologetics 93

Dealing With "Christian" Baggage. 97

Relational and Relentless Evangelism 101

Kaboom!. 105

Unleashed for THE Cause 109

Disciple Cycles 113

Call Me! It's Urgent!. 117

→ INTRO

EVANGEPHOBIA. Symptoms for this paralyzing malady include rapid heart rate, queasiness, and weakness in the knees and spine. Symptoms are triggered by even the thought of talking about Jesus with people who are not Christians. This disorder is also frequently accompanied by profuse sweating and an overpowering urge to throw up or run in the other direction.

Have you ever experienced any of these uncomfortable symptoms when a potential opportunity to share your faith comes along? If you have, you're not alone! Hundreds of thousands of teenagers like yourself find the very thought of sharing their faith with friends highly intimidating and exceedingly unnerving. Or to put it another way: It scares them to death!

But trust me, it doesn't need to be that way. With a little help, you can face down your faith-sharing fears and fuel up your passion to reach friends who need Jesus. When you learn how to talk about God naturally in normal conversations and learn how to explain the gospel in a clear, compelling way, you won't be left quaking in your Crocs™.

And that's exactly what this 30-day devotional is designed to do! Jesus has called you to share his message, and he has promised that God's Spirit will be with you every step of the way. So get ready to tackle your phobia. The real-life teenagers' stories and bite-size insights and strategies you'll find in each daily devo will help you battle back your fears and propel you forward to impact your world for Jesus.

As the teenagers in these pages attest, it's the best feeling in the whole world when you lead a friend to Christ! Are you ready to jump in? If you rely on God's Spirit for boldness, God has amazing things in store for you and your friends!

DAY 1: EVANGEWHAT?

Jesus came and told his disciples, "I have been given all authority in heaven and on earth. Therefore, go and make disciples of all the nations, baptizing them in the name of the Father and the Son and the Holy Spirit. Teach these new disciples to obey all the commands I have given you. And be sure of this: I am with you always, even to the end of the age" (Matthew 28:18-20).

THE BIG IDEA

What exactly is EVANGELISM? It's a big word for simply sharing Jesus' message of hope with a world that desperately needs him.

 LISTEN IN

"EVANGELISM really gets you out of your comfort zone, like my first experience in junior high when I was pushed out into the real world and told to go share the gospel—the coolest thing you'll ever see ever—with somebody else. And that's hard. It's the hardest thing you'll ever do. It's a mountain you have to climb every step of the way, but God is there with you. And you look down when you get to the top and see what you've accomplished and realize, whoa, that really wasn't so hard. I can totally do that again! And then that is where God really works, the second and the third time.... It gets so much easier and so much more epic every single time." —**John**

⬇ GO DEEPER

If you're going through a devotional with the title *Evangephobia*, I'm betting that the whole evangelism deal falls outside your comfort zone, just like John described in the true recounting of his own faith-sharing experience. But if you're reading a book with this title, you're also at least a bit interested in trying to figure this evangelism thing out. So good for you! After all, just the mention of the word has been known to make typically confident men and women squirm and sweat.

But I'm convinced that all the squirming and sweating among the old fogies is the result of some serious misconceptions about what evangelism is really supposed to be about. Let's face it: For many people, the word itself comes with a lot of baggage. It conjures up images of being judgmental, spouting about fire and brimstone, or pushing a particular political agenda. But that's not what Jesus has called us to be about at all. Evangelism done right is simply about sharing the best news on the planet with others—Jesus' message of hope and life.

Someone once said, "Evangelism is just one beggar showing another beggar where to find food."

Pretty simple, huh? This is the job Jesus has called all of us to in the Bible passage found at the beginning of today's devo. God calls us to spread Jesus' message and to make disciples. Making disciples means apprenticing others in the faith—and sharing our faith is the entry point for other people becoming followers of Jesus. He clearly taught that we're supposed to make him and his cause the central focus of our lives. That's why I call it THE Cause— sharing Jesus' message with others and helping them begin this journey of discipleship, too.

DO SOMETHING!

Just cracking open a book with this title shows that you're looking to push out the edges of your comfort zone a bit as you follow Jesus on this one. Way to go! This book is designed to encourage you as you face down your evangelism fears, fuel up your evangelism passion, and begin to step out and share your faith with your friends.

You're headed into a great faith-sharing adventure in the coming days, so before you jump in, spend a few minutes now writing a quick note asking God to help you as step up to this challenge.

Dear God,

HELP! You know I can't do this myself. I want to follow you, but I'm really going to need your help with this one...

_____

_____

_____

_____

_____

_____

DAY 2: FACING DOWN YOUR FEARS

Pray also for me [Paul], that whenever I speak, words may be given me so that I will fearlessly make known the mystery of the gospel (Ephesians 6:19 NIV).

 ## THE BIG IDEA

God wants to help you get past any fears you might have when it comes to sharing your faith, because God wants to do amazing things in you and through you!

 ## LISTEN IN

"It's always been on my heart to talk to him [my atheist friend] about the gospel, but I was way too wimpy to actually do it. So I was really glad that I could push myself to do it and call this friend that I'd been praying for for a really long time. I just got it into my head that I just needed to talk to him about it and not just pray for him. So I told him the story of the gospel and of Jesus. He decided that he would put his faith and trust in Jesus right then and there so that he could know for sure that he was going to heaven. So right there on the phone he prayed with me to become a Christian. It made me feel awesome! I was so excited for him! It was the coolest thing ever!"
—**Baylee**

⬇ GO DEEPER

Be honest: Are you a wimp like Baylee admitted she was for the longest time? Does just the thought of sharing your faith make you want to throw up? Relax. You're not alone. Many teenagers (and adults) have an awkward tendency to treat Jesus like an embarrassing relative that we mention to our friends only very reluctantly and with a string of apologies in tow.

But don't be discouraged—remember that even the great Apostle Peter denied Christ three times. (Check out Mark 14:66-72 if you want the whole story.) In fact, everyone from Jesus' inner circle of disciples was scared and cowered behind closed doors at one point or another. It was only through the strength and power of the Holy Spirit that they were able to get a grip, do a 180, and stand up boldly to make a difference for Jesus.

That means you're in good company. But it also means you're going to need God's strength and power in order to face your fears and share your faith. How do you tap into that strength and power? It all starts with prayer. Reread today's Bible verse at the beginning of this devo.

The request for prayer you find there was from the Apostle Paul, who was a pretty brave dude—enduring beatings, shipwreck, starvation, and prison, to name just a few of his obstacles—but even he knew he needed to pray for a fearless boldness!

 # DO SOMETHING!

Part of facing your fears is identifying what they actually are. We'll be tackling three of the most common fears in the next few devos. But right now, take a couple of minutes and make a list of your own personal, biggest fears when you think about bringing Jesus up in a conversation with your friends who don't know him.

Dear God,

I'm just saying...these are some of the things that kinda freak me out when I think about introducing my friends to you...

_____

_____

_____

_____

_____

_____

_____

_____

Still, in my best moments, I know that you are the God of the universe. Please help me tackle my fears and learn to be bold for you.

I really do want to learn how to do what you've called me to do. Would you help me with...

DAY 3: NOT COOL, MAN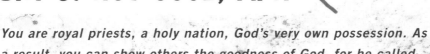

You are royal priests, a holy nation, God's very own possession. As a result, you can show others the goodness of God, for he called you out of the darkness into his wonderful light (1 Peter 2:9).

 ## THE BIG IDEA

Sometimes living for Jesus and sharing your faith can get you labeled as close-minded and hypocritical. But sharing the gospel isn't about being judgmental, it's about giving away the best gift ever—a restored relationship with a loving God.

 ## LISTEN IN

"I used to be in a gang for about three to four years. It was really a hard time to go through, losing my friends and some of my family members in that life. But since then, God has really used me, as I've actually had some of my friends and family who were in that life give their hearts to Christ….I've been challenged and mocked about my faith and teased about it at school and outside of school. But God has really made my heart strong, and he's just always there with me whenever I struggle or hear those kinds of taunts and actions toward me, saying that I'm a goodie-goodie kid or a church boy. But I take that as a compliment because, honestly, we should, because we shouldn't be ashamed of what we believe in or who we love."
—Matt

⬇ GO DEEPER

When you live for God, other people may respond in ways that surprise, shock, or disappoint you. They might judge or mock you, or they may simply not understand why you're choosing to live this way. In the middle of these moments, you can respond by demonstrating *the goodness of God*, like 1 Peter 2:9 challenges us to do. Think for a minute about ways you can display God's goodness to other people. Be creative! Here are a few ideas to get you started:

- Buy a friend a latte.

- Spend time listening to a friend who is hurting.

- Encourage someone.

- Offer to pray for someone.

- Do a good deed.

- Invite someone to lunch.

- Give a compliment.

- Mow a lawn or shovel a driveway.

- Go for ice cream with a friend—your treat.

- _____

- _____

- _____

- _____

 **DO SOMETHING!**

Now choose a few ideas that you could see yourself trying in the coming days.

1.

2.

3.

Things I learned today about displaying God's goodness to other people...

_ _

_ _

_ _

_ _

_ _

_ _

_ _

DAY 4: GET LOST!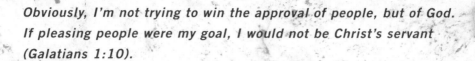

Obviously, I'm not trying to win the approval of people, but of God. If pleasing people were my goal, I would not be Christ's servant (Galatians 1:10).

THE BIG IDEA

Staying focused on Jesus will help you overcome your fear that your friends might shut you down or shut you out if you try to talk to them about spiritual things.

 LISTEN IN

"My biggest fear was losing my friends because of my faith. But I'm learning that I can share my faith without having to worry about what people think. It doesn't matter if you're cool or uncool. It doesn't matter who you are; God loves you. He's there. He cares. My faith is stronger now and I've learned that I can share my faith with even my friends who are Mormon or atheist." —**Chris**

 GO DEEPER

Do you sometimes worry that talking about Jesus with others will make you uncool?

It's true that there may be times when your friends might roll their eyes or give you the cold shoulder when you talk about Jesus. But when questioned, the vast majority of teenagers say they pray regularly to God. So why not jump in and help them better understand who God is and what God wants from them? The key is to remember that the benefits to them are HUGE—starting right now with the hope and meaning that come from a restored relationship with God and lasting throughout eternity in heaven.

And remember, if you find yourself facing a chilly reception, take comfort in knowing that as hard as it may feel, pleasing God is more important than pleasing people.

 # DO SOMETHING!

Have a conversation with God right now about how you're feeling about the potential of your friends telling you to "get lost!"

Dear God,

The possibility that my friends might reject me if I start trying to talk to them about you has me feeling kinda anxious. Please help me stay focused on you and help me get my heart around the truth that it's more important to please you than it is to please people. I could really use your help with this...

DAY 5: SAY WHAT?

If you need wisdom, ask our generous God, and he will give it to you. He will not rebuke you for asking (James 1:5)

 ## THE BIG IDEA

Not knowing what to say can make sharing your faith a stomach-churning endeavor, but there are lots of ways to naturally integrate God into conversations with your friends.

 ## LISTEN IN

"**THE CAUSE** [sharing our faith and making disciples who make disciples] is what we need to do; there's no way to get around it. It's everything! It's urgent! It's what we need to do! There's no other way to describe it. But my fear is that I'll push my friends away, and then I won't be able to talk to them again about it—because a lot of my friends, if they hear something they don't like, they'll just leave. So I'm scared of wording it wrong and scaring them away." —**Ryan**

 ## GO DEEPER

Many teenagers are fearful they won't know what to say if they try to talk about Jesus with their friends. After all, God's a big subject.

Where do you start?

Actually, the starting possibilities are almost endless. There are tons of ways to bring God into your conversations. Figuring out what's a fit for you will help you overcome this fear. In my experience, there are four basic approaches to initiating spiritual conversations:

Creative:

- Have you ever wondered about God?

- What do you think God wants from you?

- Would it surprise you to know that God wants a relationship with you that starts now and lasts forever?

Direct:

- Where are you when it comes to God and religion?

- What's your religious background?

- Can I tell you why I believe it's all about a relationship with God and not about following a religion?

Relational:

- Would you mind telling me about yourself and what's important to you?

- Would you tell me about your spiritual journey so far?

- I've been wondering, can you share with me your view of God?

Logical:

- Who do you think Jesus was—truly God, a good teacher, or something else? Why do you think that?

- What do you believe about God, and why?

- Why do you think there are so many different religions? Do you think they can all be right?

These are just a few examples of opening questions to get your own creative juices flowing. So think about what might work best for you and your style of relating. Your confidence will grow as you figure out the approach that's right for you.

Of course, after you get the God-talk initiated with some opening questions, your job is to listen. You'll learn a lot about where your friends are coming from spiritually. And eventually there will come a point where you will be able to share your own faith story and talk about what you believe. At that stage it will be important to know how to present the gospel in a clear and compelling way. But no worries on that front—we'll get to that in the days ahead.

 # DO SOMETHING!

Spend some time alone thinking through these opening questions and writing some additional questions that reflect you and your style of relating. Think about how the conversation might flow as you ask and listen. Make a note here of which questions feel like the best fit for you.

Opening questions I want to try...

DAY 6: THE ANTIDOTE

After this prayer, the meeting place shook, and they were all filled with the Holy Spirit. Then they preached the word of God with boldness (Acts 4:31).

THE BIG IDEA

Prayer conquers fear! So pray! Pray for boldness to overcome your fears. Pray for wisdom to know what to say. Pray for your friends who need Jesus.

LISTEN IN

"As I started thinking and praying about who God wanted me to share my faith with, he didn't just give me one person. He gave me 20—all the guys on my soccer team, and there are only two other Christians. So it's a huge step and a risky one. But I know God is large and in charge and that he will speak through me." —**Jamie**

GO DEEPER

Conquering your fears must start with prayer.

God stands ready to help you in this faith-sharing journey if you just ask. God will sweep into your life with his strength, passion, wisdom, and power! You see, while it's your job to be faithful to Christ's call to participate in his search-and-rescue mission to reach people who don't know Jesus, it's the job of God's Spirit's to move hearts and souls and call them *out of the darkness into his wonderful light (1 Peter 2:9).*

If you feel fear rising, let it remind you to pray. Rest in the confidence of knowing that God loves and longs to reach your friends who need Jesus! God's totally in this with you.

So face down your EVANGELISM fears with prayer.

 # DO SOMETHING!

Pray for wisdom to know what to say. Pray down your fears. Pray for boldness to overcome your fears. Then ask God to bring to mind one friend that you know needs Jesus. Write down that friend's name and begin praying for God to start working in that person's heart right now to be ready to hear more about God.

Dear God,

My friend, _____, really needs to get to know you...

_____

_____

_____

_____

DAY 7: YOUR WEAKNESS =
GOD'S STRENGTH

Each time he said, "My grace is all you need. My power works best in weakness." So now I am glad to boast about my weaknesses, so that the power of Christ can work through me. That's why I take pleasure in my weaknesses, and in the insults, hardships, persecutions, and troubles that I suffer for Christ. For when I am weak, then I am strong (2 Corinthians 12:9-10).

 ## THE BIG IDEA

God doesn't need perfect people to spread his message. God delights in using those who are imperfect and fully dependent on him for their self-esteem, strength, and wisdom.

 ## LISTEN IN

"I was holding out. And my mistake could cost my friend the chance of ever getting to experience the joy of knowing God. That night I wrote my best friend a letter and I was just in tears by the end of the letter because there was so much to say. The next week, I gave her the letter. I was so incredibly nervous about it because she is a very strong atheist and is not very open-minded, but God gave me the strength to give it to her anyway....I know that that letter did mean something to her even if she did not choose that moment to give her life over to Christ. God guarded my heart, and because of that I am so much more confident in my faith. He has never steered me wrong, and I know he never will." —**Ashley**

 ## GO DEEPER

Sometimes Christians think they need to be picture-perfect before they can step out and talk to others about their own faith. Now reread the verses at the beginning of this devo.

Do you need to be perfect to talk about God with your friends? NO!

God delights in using the unlikely and unassuming to accomplish great things for him. Throughout the Bible we see God using young, inexperienced people in mighty ways: a teenage shepherd boy named David conquered Goliath and saved his nation; the young Queen Esther saved the entire Jewish race; and Mary, Jesus' mother, was a simple teenage girl whose humble response to God's call on her life changed the course of history.

God is in the business of doing great things through ordinary people who are completely committed to him—including ordinary teenagers. That's why God wants to use you to reach your generation in spite of your weaknesses and inexperience. Who better to reach teenagers than other teenagers? Who better to reach your broken and hurting friends than you? Remember, it's all about "one beggar showing another beggar where to find food." You're offering Christ to your friends, not some holier-than-thou, plastic, cookie-cutter, man-made religion.

🎧 DO SOMETHING!

God wants to use you to reach your friends in the midst of your authentic, genuine relationship with them. Today, nurture your relationship with a friend who doesn't know Jesus by doing something generous. Go back to your brainstorm list from Day 3 to jog your memory about some possible ideas. Take a minute and talk to God about your friend and your plan before you set it in motion.

Dear God,

I'm thinking about my friend, _____, who really needs to get to know you. Please help prepare my friend's heart to hear about you. I'm going to try to do something generous for my friend today, and I'm hoping that will begin to help my friend get a glimpse of you in my life and my actions so that my friend will be ready to hear about you when I'm ready to initiate a spiritual conversation...

_____

_____

_____

_____

_____

DAY 8: FUELING YOUR PASSION

"For the Son of Man came to seek and save those who are lost"
(Luke 19:10).

 ## THE BIG IDEA

Jesus was passionate about seeking and saving spiritually hungry people. We should be, too!

 ## LISTEN IN

"There's this girl I've kinda been talking with lately, and she's never really known Christ; she kinda has a void in her life. She's been abused and mistreated emotionally a lot. And I started discussing Christ with her....It was just a really cool experience. I feel like I've really been used by God to do something helpful and maybe change somebody's life and now maybe I'll have the opportunity to reach more lives. It's a cool experience. It's like God's really using you when you do it, and it just feels really cool." —**Jacob**

 ## GO DEEPER

When you think about it, a variety of passions can motivate you and fuel your drive to excel at something—whether it's sports, music, academics, or whatever. These motivations can range from popularity to getting a scholarship to hearing your coach or teacher say "good job" to pleasing your parents or helping your team, band, or family.

In the same way, I believe God has provided different **EVANGELISM** "passion fuels" to help energize your efforts to share your faith. Without a passion to share your faith, you won't be motivated to learn how to do it effectively and you'll most likely be tempted to bail at the first sign of difficulty.

Having a heart that burns and breaks for people—just like Jesus had—is what will keep you sharing with others for the long haul.

I've identified several different types of passion fuel that can keep you motivated to share Jesus' message. Over the next four days, we'll be taking a look at some of these fuels.

 # DO SOMETHING!

Spend some time asking God to give you a heart that's growing in its passion for reaching people in your life who are far from God. Pray for a growing passion to reach your friends who need Jesus. Only God can ignite the love and passion you need to hang in there through the ups and downs of this faith-sharing journey.

Dear God,

Jesus was passionate about seeking and saving people. I want to be passionate, too. But I'm not there yet. So I need your help. Please work in my heart and give me a growing passion to reach my lost friends.

I want to expand my list of friends I'm going to try to reach with your message. So right now I want to talk to you about these three friends who need Jesus.

1.

2.

3.

DAY 9: OBEDIENCE 101

For we must all stand before Christ to be judged. We will each receive whatever we deserve for the good or evil we have done in this earthly body. Because we understand our fearful responsibility to the Lord, we work hard to persuade others. God knows we are sincere, and I hope you know this, too (2 Corinthians 5:10-11).

 ## THE BIG IDEA

It's plain and simple: Jesus said, "Go and make disciples." So we should go do it.

 ## LISTEN IN

"I had a friend who texted me; she hadn't texted me in a while. I knew she'd been through some problems lately....She said, "I'm really bored." I said, "I have a great idea. Let's talk about the relationships we have with God." And she said, "*&$#, no, I'll pass." And I'm like, "Well, what's so wrong about talking about it?" She's like, "Well, I'm atheist." And I said, "Well, alright." Then I asked her, "Why do you choose to be atheist?" And she's all, "Just leave me alone, weirdo." And it just clicked in my head: This must be one of those uncool things—being uncool. And I just got excited and then I told her, "Well, what's wrong with believing that after I die I'm going to have everlasting life with God?" And she's all just, "Leave me alone, OK? I don't want to talk about it." And I said, "I'll still be praying for you." And she said, "Don't bother praying for me anymore." But I'm still going to. —**Bryan**

GO DEEPER

Jesus told us to do it. So we should do it. Case closed. For some Christians, this is all the motivation it takes to get into gear and share the gospel with others. Knowing you will one day stand before God and give an account can definitely fuel your passion to obey Jesus' command to go and make disciples. (Check out 1 Corinthians 3:13-15 to learn more.)

Still, it's important to be clear: Sharing your faith isn't something you do to earn your way to heaven. Your salvation comes as a free gift because of what Jesus did on the cross. The grace and forgiveness God offers is an unearned gift; all you have to do to receive it is trust in Jesus alone for your salvation.

Sharing your faith out of obedience is something you do out of your relationship with God because you're committed to following God. After all, God is the Lord of the universe, so we should all seriously listen to what we are instructed to do. God knows what is best for us, and we are called to do things that help accomplish God's purposes and make us into the people we are intended to be. Obedience is about trusting that God knows what is best for our lives.

Sharing our faith is a part of our journey of growing and experiencing the fullness of what God has for us. We are God's chosen method of reaching a hurting world.

📸 DO SOMETHING!

Since the beginning of time (think Adam and Eve here), obedience has come hard for humans. Why is that?

Using the following prompts, spend some time today wrestling with that question today.

Three reasons why I ought to obey God and share my faith...

1.

2.

3.

Three reasons why I sometimes don't feel like actually doing it...

1.

2.

3.

Then have a talk with God about your insights, and ask God for help.

DAY 10: LOVE, LOVE, LOVE

Jesus replied, " 'You must love the Lord your God with all your heart, all your soul, and all your mind.' This is the first and greatest commandment. A second is equally important: 'Love your neighbor as yourself.' The entire law and all the demands of the prophets are based on these two commandments" (Matthew 22:37-40).

 ## THE BIG IDEA

Your love for God and your love for others can fuel your passion to share your faith.

 ## LISTEN IN

"No matter what you've gone through or who you are, there's still a God out there who loves you. It just blows me away every time I hear it....I went to my school and went up to all my friends and told them all about Christ, whether they accepted it or not. It was interesting listening to some of things people said about it....You always hear people talk about, "If you believe in Jesus and everything, that's dumb. Why would you believe in something you can't see, you can't feel, you can't touch?" Well, in the Bible it says that your belief is based off your faith. And believing in something you can't see takes a lot of faith. But just being called uncool—it's worth it....That's fine, I believe and I'll keep talking about it whether you like it or not. Because it's what I believe and what I love and I know it's the truth and it's real. Why would you hide something from people that could save them?" —**Jared**

 # GO DEEPER

God's love for you and your love for God are things you cannot keep to yourself.

Think about it. You talk about what you love with those you love. It's only natural. If you love a particular food or have a favorite movie, your friends know about it, right? It's the same thing with your relationship with God. Your friends should know about it—including those who don't currently have a relationship with Jesus.

And true love inspires sacrifice. God loved you enough to suffer and die for you. You can demonstrate your love for him by stepping out and sharing his message whether or not your friends think it's uncool. Like Jared said, "It's worth it....Because it's what I believe and what I love and I know it's the truth and it's real. Would you hide something from people that could save them?"

So let your love for God and for others motivate you to share the best news ever with everyone who needs to hear it!

 # DO SOMETHING!

Do you talk about the God you love with your friends? Or are there people in your life who don't even know that you're a Christian? Maybe you've sometimes treated Jesus like an embarrassing relative that you don't particularly want to introduce around. It's time to get over yourself and step out bravely.

As you interact with people today, look for opportunities to naturally talk about the fact that you're a follower of Jesus. Circle one of the following ideas that you want to try using today to do this. Or feel free to come up with your own unique approach.

- Tell a story about something that happened recently at church or youth group.

- Share a way you saw God at work in the world today.

- Comment on the beauty of God's creation—a sunset, a flower, a tree, a pet, a person.

- Offer a God-focused explanation about why you don't drink, do drugs, or sleep around.

- Talk about your plans for the future and how you're praying about a decision that's ahead.

- Put in a good word for Jesus.

God, help me to grow in love for others, especially for these individuals...

DAY 11: THEY NEED JESUS NOW! ←

When he saw the crowds, he had compassion on them because they were confused and helpless, like sheep without a shepherd. He said to his disciples, "The harvest is great, but the workers are few. So pray to the Lord who is in charge of the harvest; ask him to send more workers into his fields" (Matthew 9:36-38).

THE BIG IDEA

Compassion for people—seeing the hell your friends are going through right now—can motivate you to share Jesus' love and hope with them.

 LISTEN IN

"Over the summer I fell into a lot of bad peer pressures; I don't know, like stuff that makes you cool, you know, whatever your friends want to do—parties and all that. One day, one of my friends that I hadn't connected with in years texted me—he got my number on Facebook®—and he asked me if I wanted to hang out. I said sure. So he took me to his youth group, and I gotta say that his simple invitation was one of the biggest changes ever in my life! I've trusted Christ, and I'm growing closer to God, and my life is so much better with God. I need God in my life." —**Dan**

 GO DEEPER

You know it's true: As a friend you have a lot more influence on your own friends than any stranger ever could. You see friend influence coming through loud and clear in Dan's story above—first the bad influence and then the good. Influence runs both ways. Peer pressure pushed him into partying, and then a Christian friend from his distant past extended a simple invitation to youth group.

This kind of peer influence that every teenager knows about instinctively has actually been studied by the "experts," like sociologists and psychologists. And the experts have confirmed that friends have significantly more influence on their friends than strangers do.

So when you see friends hurting or heading down the wrong path, don't just let it tug at your heart and make you feel bad for them. Step up and share the hope you have in Jesus, encourage them to check God out, and, since their life without God isn't working so great for them, challenge them to explore how life with God might be a better way. Let your compassion fuel your faith-sharing passion.

But there's no need to wait for a crisis moment; the hope you have in Jesus is news too good to keep to yourself.

 DO SOMETHING!

Pray about it, and then invite a friend who needs Jesus to go to church or youth group with you this week. You never know; a simple invitation out of the blue to hang out may morph into a visit to youth group, which may turn your friend's life upside down in a good way, just like it did for Dan.

God, thanks for these people who have influenced me to find you and grow in my faith...

DAY 12: ETERNITY IS A LOOOONG TIME

And just as each person is destined to die once and after that comes judgment, so also Christ died once for all time as a sacrifice to take away the sins of many people. He will come again, not to deal with our sins, but to bring salvation to all who are eagerly waiting for him (Hebrews 9:27-28).

 ## THE BIG IDEA

The eternal realities of heaven and hell can fuel your passion to share your faith and bring urgency to your efforts.

 ## LISTEN IN

"A while back I took up the challenge to share my faith. I knew immediately who I wanted to share with—one of my best friends, Sarah. We'd been friends since we were 9, but I'd never talked about God with her. So I called her and shared the gospel with her. The next day she told me that she believed!

A few short months later a very difficult phone call came. Sarah had died suddenly from a massive brain aneurysm. That was the hardest day of my life. I can't describe how angry I was at God. But I remembered the phone call I'd initiated a few months earlier. It has made all the difference. I will always miss my friend, and it still hurts very much, but I have a reason to smile whenever I think of her. We will be together forever in heaven!

I can't tell you how urgent it is that you share your faith with your friends, because you never know when it might be too late."
—**Megan**

 # GO DEEPER

It's natural to want the assurance that your friends and loved ones will be with you someday in heaven. It provides great hope and comfort when you know that you'll be spending all eternity together in a place of great joy and celebration—the ultimate, unending party scene in the presence of the God of the universe. Desiring the assurance of your friends' salvation can be a great motivator for reaching them with the gospel message. But this is about more than just feeling good because you know they'll be with you. This is about impacting someone's destiny for all eternity—heaven or hell.

Everybody loves the idea of heaven. Hell, not so much. Frankly, the very concept of hell has fallen out of favor in recent years. It's so unpleasant and unsettling—and sounds so judgmental.

So even though the doctrine of hell might make your brain hurt and your heart ache, Scripture refers to it in black and white again and again. No matter how you try to imagine it away or tone it down, one thing is clear, the Bible describes hell as for real and forever—your worst fears come true and then multiplied by infinity for eternity.

Don't run away from these eternal realities; instead, let them fuel your passion to share your faith and let them bring urgency to your efforts.

Because like Megan said, "you never know when it might be too late."

 # DO SOMETHING!

Launch into a spiritual conversation today with one of the three friends you listed back on Day 8 by broaching the subject of what happens when we die. Try using one of the following conversation starters, or come up with one of your own.

- Did you hear about that _____ (accident, death, illness, tragedy)? What do you think happens when we die?

- Ever wonder about whether there's an afterlife?

- Take a survey of your friends on Facebook® and find out who believes what: heaven/hell, reincarnation, extinction, or something else.

Things I learned today about launching a spiritual conversation with a friend...

DAY 13: DISCOVERING YOUR PASSION FUEL

"But you will receive power when the Holy Spirit comes upon you. And you will be my witnesses, telling people about me everywhere—in Jerusalem, throughout Judea, in Samaria, and to the ends of the earth" (Acts 1:8).

 ## THE BIG IDEA

Discovering which particular passion fuel best fills your own evangelism tank can help you stay motivated to share your faith with friends.

 ## LISTEN IN

"I texted my brother Sean. And when I got a hold of him, I spent a good half hour talking to him and asking him where he was in his faith. And I got him to agree to come over and talk to me a little bit more about it. For his entire life he's felt like he doesn't really know God, and he wants to believe, but he doesn't know exactly what's up there or if there is anything up there. But when I talked to him I just felt like there was a true bond and that I could really help him find his way, and it was just meaningful and heartfelt, and I'm just gonna be there for whoever needs it and help them find their way. I'm living THE Cause [sharing our faith and making disciples who make disciples] and I'm going to share it." **—Sydney**

 **GO DEEPER**

Sydney's passion fuel is compassion for the lost. She wants to help others find their way to Jesus. Like Sydney, when you discover your evangelism passion fuel, you'll be come more focused in your outreach efforts and you'll see God start to use you in amazing ways to further the kingdom. And that's an awesome feeling.

You may have one distinct passion fuel that motivates you above all others, or you may find that a combination of several fits you best. But whichever mix works for you, fuel up on a regular basis by revisiting your overriding motivations as you're praying for your friends. And then work to add more types of passion fuel into your mix. After all, if you look at Jesus' life, he blended several different motivations together.

But regardless of your passion fuel blend, whether you're totally new at this faith-sharing thing or you've done it a dozen times or more, it pretty much always starts with stepping out and being willing to talk about God with your friends. So ask God to fuel you up, then turn on your "faith-sharing radar" and look for opportunities to turn the conversation toward spiritual topics.

 **DO SOMETHING!**

Go back to the conversation-starting questions from Day 5 and review the ones you'd selected to try sometime. Now it's time to roll them out for the real deal.

Pray and ask God to help you spot at least one opportunity today to initiate a spiritual conversation with someone who doesn't know Jesus yet. Then activate your faith-sharing radar, and go for it with all the passion God has given you.

At this point, I think my primary passion fuel is
_____, and here's why...

DAY 14: RELIGION VS. RELATIONSHIP

I pray that from his glorious, unlimited resources he will empower you with inner strength through his Spirit. Then Christ will make his home in your hearts as you trust in him. Your roots will grow down into God's love and keep you strong. And may you have the power to understand, as all God's people should, how wide, how long, how high, and how deep his love is. May you experience the love of Christ, though it is too great to understand fully. Then you will be made complete with all the fullness of life and power that comes from God (Ephesians 3:16-19).

THE BIG IDEA

The gospel is all about a relationship with God and not about a set of religious rules. Help your friends understand that you are encouraging them to trust in Jesus Christ—a person.

 LISTEN IN

"I had an experience in a class with a friend where we got on the subject of religion. I told him that I really didn't like using the word religion, because I had a relationship with God. He kinda asked me more about what the relationship was. So I told him my background of being a Christian and having a relationship with God, and I asked him, "What do you believe? What's your mindset on this?" And he actually told me that he was a Wiccan and that he believed in "the lord and the lady" and things like that. It was funny, because our youth group had just got done watching the *GOSPEL Journey Adventure* where they had a Wiccan on there, so I knew some background of where he was coming from and stuff that I could say and ask him.

We had about a half hour of talking, and he said, "Man, this is an eye-opener. God has really sent you to me so I can realize this. It's so much better!" So we had lunch next, and he and I walked outside, sat on a park bench, and I shared my faith and went over the gospel with him. I wound up leading him to Christ, which was the coolest thing ever…to be the guy that God used—it's awesome. You read that stuff in the Bible and you don't think it's going to happen to you. And for it to happen to you, it's like, wow, God's really out there, and he really wants to use me." —**Colin**

 # GO DEEPER

Reread Colin's story above, this time from the perspective of the friend he led to Christ. What contributed to Colin's friend trusting in Jesus? A thirst for something more and the draw of a relationship with God. You hear it in the guy's words when he said, "Man, this is an eye-opener. God has really sent you to me so I can realize this. It's so much better!"

All it took was someone like Colin simply taking the time and making the effort to talk to his friend about entering into a relationship with Jesus. It's the intimate God-relationship dimension of the gospel that sets it apart from all other religious worldviews floating around out there.

DO SOMETHING!

Spend some time thinking about the difference between following a set of religious rules and having a relationship with God. Write down some of your thoughts.

Following a set of religious rules looks like this:

- Do this...

- Don't do that...

- Can I ever measure up...

- What will people think if...

- _____

- _____

- _____

Being in a relationship looks like this...

- I love you because...

- I want to spend time with you by...

- I think you're awesome because...

- I want what you want, which is...

- _____

- _____

- _____

Things I learned today about the difference between following a set of religious rules and being in a relationship with God...

DAY 15: BC: BEFORE CHRIST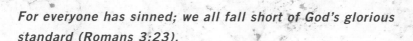

For everyone has sinned; we all fall short of God's glorious standard (Romans 3:23).

 ## THE BIG IDEA

Talking to your friends about your own personal faith story can serve as an invitation for others to check out Jesus. Sharing your own story starts with describing what your life was like before you trusted in Jesus.

 ## LISTEN IN

"You don't need to have had a horrible life before you trusted Christ to give a testimony, because we're all sinners....It's actually more beautiful when you see someone who's been fulfilled in Jesus Christ for most of their life. They haven't needed to go through all that pain and suffering, looking for fulfillment in all those destructive things like drugs and alcohol and sex. When you find satisfaction in Jesus, people will be so curious that it kills them inside—that's what happened to me, people loved me and God took a hold of my heart and ripped all that stuff out of my life so that he could redeem me."
—**Andrew**

GO DEEPER

Your faith story is often called a "testimony." But I like to call it "The Before and After Factor." It's simply sharing with others in three simple stages:

1. What your life was like before you trusted Jesus.

2. The factors that contributed to you putting your trust in Jesus.

3. What your life's been like since you trusted Jesus.

Communicating your own personal faith story is an important part of sharing Jesus with your friends because real-life stories grab people's attention and move hearts. But sharing your story effectively takes some preparation. That's why it's a good idea to think through your faith journey so you are prepared to succinctly describe it to others in a clear, compelling way.

The before phase of your story should address questions like: What did you struggle with? How did you feel? What were you looking for?

Keep in mind that you don't have to have a traumatic background—like being a drug addict or a juvenile delinquent—to have an engaging faith story. As Andrew pointed out, being raised in a Christian home and living a life that's been committed to Jesus for as long as you can remember is actually the most beautiful of all faith stories, because you didn't need to be scarred or damaged by the ravages of a sin-filled experience.

 # DO SOMETHING!

Preparing your testimony is not some self-absorbed exercise in being the center of attention or showing off how wonderful your life is. Sharing your faith journey should be done in humility. So keep it real. Be authentic.

Over these next few devos, you'll be crafting a brief summary of your own faith journey. We'll break it down into the three simple stages. Today, work on the first part of your story, the before phase. Spend some time writing a two- or three-sentence summary of what your life was like before you had a relationship with Jesus. (If you can't remember back to a point when you didn't trust Christ, you probably faced a moment when you decided to make the faith you had been raised in your own, so feel free to use that as the pivotal dividing point in your spiritual journey that separates your before and after experiences.)

My life before Jesus...

DAY 16: THE FACTOR: WHAT OPENED YOUR EYES?

You were dead because of your sins and because your sinful nature was not yet cut away. Then God made you alive with Christ, for he forgave all our sins. He canceled the record of the charges against us and took it away by nailing it to the cross (Colossians 2:13-14).

 ## THE BIG IDEA

By telling your friends about the experiences, emotions, or people that were instrumental in opening your eyes to the truth of the gospel, you're inviting them to consider Jesus, too.

 ## LISTEN IN

"Although I was sitting in the crowded school library, I felt all alone. I was miserable and guilt-ridden because I had recently stabbed myself to kill the baby growing inside me. Although my body had recovered from this self-inflicted wound, my soul was a mess. My hopeless, helpless feelings overwhelmed me, and I couldn't stop crying there in the library in front of everyone.

But then a girl named Theresa stopped and sat down beside me and asked me what was wrong. She listened. Then she told me that she, too, knew what it was like to live in guilt and despair, but had found a better way. She explained the gospel story to me and told me how God still loved me and that I could be forgiven through Jesus Christ.

So that day in the middle of the library, with tears flowing, I became a child of God. I now know that my sins are forgiven and that one day I will meet my baby on the other side of eternity. Theresa took the time to reach out to me when everybody else just passed me by, and what she told me changed my life." —**M**

 # GO DEEPER

The second part of the "Before and After Factor" is describing the people or experiences that pointed you to Jesus. It's easy to see the factors in M's story that played a pivotal role in her accepting Christ. Everyone's faith story is different, so yours may look very different from M's.

Here are some of the more common faith factors that the Holy Spirit uses to bring people to a point of faith:

- Guilt over past wrongs

- Wanting to go to heaven or not wanting to go to hell

- Thirsting for something more

- The need for purpose and significance

Regardless of the emotional ups and downs of life that often contribute to preparing someone to consider Jesus, most everyone's faith factors include an experience where someone like Theresa simply took the time and made the effort to talk about Jesus and explain the gospel.

 # DO SOMETHING!

What were your faith factors? A particular spiritual conversation? A struggle? A camp? Whatever it was, as you tell about your own faith story, find a way to communicate the life-changing faith factors that the Holy Spirit used to point you toward trusting in Jesus alone.

Write out a two- or three-sentence summary of the people, emotions, or experiences that were influential in pointing you toward the truth of the gospel.

The faith factors that caused me to trust in Jesus...

_____

_____

_____

_____

_____

_____

_____

_____

Now, maybe you've been reading this section and aren't sure about your own relationship with God. As the Bible says, *Today is the day of salvation (2 Corinthians 6:2)*. In other words, why wait? Make sure you have a relationship with God by believing the GOSPEL? What is the GOSPEL?

God created us to be with him.

Our sins separate us from God.

Sins cannot be removed by good deeds.

Paying the price for sin, Jesus died and rose again.

Everyone who trusts in Jesus alone has eternal life.

Life with Jesus starts now and lasts forever.

If you've just put your faith and trust in Jesus, you can say this simple prayer to God as an expression of your faith:

"Dear God, I know I'm a sinner. But I believe that Jesus died for me on the cross and rose from the dead. I trust in him alone to forgive me for my sins and to give me eternal life. I receive it right now through faith alone in Jesus alone. Thank you so much for this wonderful gift!"

DAY 17: AFTER CHRIST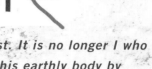

My old self has been crucified with Christ. It is no longer I who live, but Christ lives in me. So I live in this earthly body by trusting in the Son of God, who loved me and gave himself for me (Galatians 2:20).

 ## THE BIG IDEA

Authentically sharing about what your life is like now that you've trusted Jesus can help your friends understand what a relationship with God is all about.

 ## LISTEN IN

"Last year I wrecked my car and I ended up breaking my back, and now I'm paralyzed from the waist down. Before this happened, I never really went to church...but since, I've learned that God didn't put me in this wheelchair, but that he allows me to be in this wheelchair, and that he allows me to teach others that with faith and trust in him, I can move on with my life. There's life outside of this, and I'm not really too worried about whether I'll ever walk again or not. I'm definitely not going to be afraid to share my faith anymore. I've been terrified to talk to people; I'm a shy person, but I've learned that if I can make it through a car accident, then I can definitely make it through sharing my faith with somebody else. God really does have a plan for you. Never doubt it. If he brought you to it, he'll bring you through it" —**Courtney**

GO DEEPER

The third part of the "Before and After Factor" involves communicating what your life is like since you've trusted in Christ. How is it different? What has changed? What have you left behind? What have you gained? How do you feel now that you are in a relationship with God, who is personally concerned about you and actively involved in your life? What does it feel like to walk with God through the ups and downs of life?

Life isn't always smooth sailing just because you're a Christian.

The difference comes in knowing that God loves you and that because you've put your trust in Christ alone for your salvation, God has saved you from an eternity worse than just physical death. Knowing that God promises to never abandon you (see Hebrews 13:5-6) no matter the road ahead makes all the difference in the world.

DO SOMETHING!

Spend a few minutes right now and write out a two- or three-sentence summary of what your life is like now that you've put your faith and trust in Jesus and have a personal relationship with him.

My life now that I've trusted in Jesus...

DAY 18: DARE 2 SHARE YOUR STORY

This means that anyone who belongs to Christ has become a new person. The old life is gone; a new life has begun! (2 Corinthians 5:17).

 ## THE BIG IDEA

Your personal faith story can serve as an invitation for your friends to check Jesus out.

 ## LISTEN IN

"I didn't like who I was, so I decided to 'fix' myself. I thought that if I could be pretty enough, people would see some worth in me. So I starved myself to get to that 'beautiful' person I thought would be there if I got down to 98 lbs....But that didn't satisfy, so in my desperation to feel wanted, I went online and found "worth" from guys. Somehow along the way I mixed up love and lust.

After a while, I just started to feel numb, and during this numbness I ran into something that relieved it a bit. I found cutting. As I would stand in my bathroom and watch the blood run, it was strangely comforting. Because it was proof to me that I was living, I was alive. I lived this way for two years. That was my life. And even though I was scared to death, I didn't see any way out.

My life-changing moment came at a Dare 2 Share conference, when they had us pull out a paper we had written our "greatest sin" on. As we tore it up as a symbol of Christ forgiving our greatest sins, I just started to cry. I was bawling my eyes out, because I truly felt like I was laying things before the cross. For the first time in a long time, I felt loved and I felt wanted. And that just overwhelmed me. I prayed then that Christ would truly take over my life, and he did. I still have my troubles, but I've learned to lean on him to get through them.

My life changed. Truly changed. I am living every day I can for Christ. God revealed himself to me and my life changed, and I have not been the same since. I went from an anorexic, porn-addicted cutter, to a born-again, set-ablaze believer. Christ has the power to change lives, even today. I am living proof." —**Taylor**

 ## GO DEEPER

There's power in Taylor's transforming story. The "Before and After Factor" are clearly laid out for all to see. I'm sure that some of you are thinking right now that your own faith story isn't dramatic enough to be of interest to anyone. I beg to differ. While some have a more dramatic before story and some have a more dramatic after story, absolutely everyone has a dramatic midpoint in their story. That point when God *called you out of the darkness into his wonderful light (1 Peter 2:9)* is an incredible, transforming event in your life and one that would be selfish to keep to yourself!

 ## DO SOMETHING!

Now pull it all together—the before, the faith factor, and the after. Practice explaining it in a short simple story form. Then call or hang out with a Christian friend and try it out on them.

Ask for honest feedback and any suggestions—because tomorrow you'll be taking your story on the road and telling it to someone who's not a follower of Christ.

Based on all three sections, my faith story is...

_____

_____

_____

_____

_____

_____

_____

_____

_____

_____

DAY 19: GOD WANTS TO USE YOU!

Then, calling the crowd to join his disciples, he [Jesus] said, "If any of you wants to be my follower, you must turn from your selfish ways, take up your cross, and follow me. If you try to hang on to your life, you will lose it. But if you give up your life for my sake and for the sake of the Good News, you will save it" (Mark 8:34-35).

 ## THE BIG IDEA

God wants to use you and your faith story to reach others with the good news of Jesus.

 ## LISTEN IN

"I can't believe it, but on Saturday God used me to touch four lives! And three accepted Christ! And yesterday I got to talk to some of the girls on my soccer team about my faith because of the shirt I was wearing....I'm all in!" —**Emily**

 ## GO DEEPER

Throughout the pages of this devotional, you've read stories of real teenagers who dared to share their faith. But behind the scenes, every one of those stories started when a teenager stepped out and brought God up in conversation.

One of the best ways to bring God up in conversation is to start with some opening questions. (Review Day 5 for ideas.) Try to get your friends talking about what they believe. Most people like to share their beliefs and opinions. Listen carefully, ask follow-up questions, interact, and discuss. Then ask your friends if you can share your own faith story with them. This is your opportunity to talk to them about how important God is in your life. Who can argue with that?

Granted, they may shut you down. But no one can argue with your own personal experience of God. That's why it can serve as a good bridge builder for deeper spiritual discussion.

 DO SOMETHING!

So pray, pray, pray. Ask God to help you face down your fears. Ask for courage and boldness, like the Apostle Paul did. Ask God to prepare the hearts of your friends, and dare to share your story.

Pick an opening question and jump into a spiritual conversation today with one of your three friends who need Jesus (look back at Day 8 for the list you created). Look for an opportunity to share the faith story you've been preparing and practicing over these past few days. If you need a transition to open the way for sharing your story, try something like: "Hey, I have this assignment where I'm supposed to talk to someone about my spiritual journey. Can I just quickly run it by you and get your feedback about whether the way I'm explaining it makes sense? I'd really like to know what you think."

How I felt today about sharing my faith story with a friend...

_____

_____

DAY 20: DARE 2 SHARE
JESUS' STORY

" 'I'm sending you off to open the eyes of the outsiders so they can see the difference between dark and light, and choose light, see the difference between Satan and God, and choose God. I'm sending you off to present my offer of sins forgiven, and a place in the family, inviting them into the company of those who begin real living by believing in me' " (Acts 26:17-18 The Message).

 ## THE BIG IDEA

While your faith story can be powerfully moving, Jesus' story is the Ultimate Story.

 ## LISTEN IN

"On the school bus I've had the opportunity to share the gospel with four or five different students, and one girl, Keisha, decided to follow Christ. My sharing was brought up through various conversations and was all quite informal. There were times of great debate on the school bus about what the Bible says and what Jesus actually did. I had several atheists who shared the back seats of the bus with me off and on....I think it was on the back of that school bus that I learned to reach out to others and to stand up for what I believe."
—Elisabeth

GO DEEPER ←

Sharing your own personal faith story is a very relational lead-in to sharing the gospel with your friends who need Jesus. But there's more to sharing your faith than just sharing your own faith story. You also need to be ready to share the Ultimate Story, which is Jesus' story—the gospel story.

Your personal experience can be powerful and engaging, but in order for your friends to put their faith and trust in Jesus, they need to understand the gospel message. It's the gospel message explained in the pages of the Bible that will help them get a glimpse of who God is, what God is like, and the truth that God wants a relationship with them. The gospel communicates the truth about a God who is worth trusting in and following after.

But many teenagers feel overwhelmed at the thought of trying to explain the major plotline of the Bible to their friends. After all, the Bible's a big book and God's a big topic. How do you begin to explain the grand, sweeping story of God's interaction with humans and God's desire for a deep, personal relationship with each and every one of us?

I've found that it helps if you think about sharing the gospel with someone as a "journey" through major themes of the Bible with a few key stops along the way. A short, simple, six-letter acrostic that spells out the word "GOSPEL" summarizes these core essentials. It's called the GOSPEL Journey® Message and it goes like this.

> **G**od **created us to be with him.**
> *Know that the Lord is God. It is he who made us, and we are his; we are his people, the sheep of his pasture (Psalm 100:3 NIV).*
>
> **O**ur **sins separate us from God.**
> *For all have sinned and fall short of the glory of God (Romans 3:23 NIV).*

Sins cannot be removed by good deeds.
All of us have become like one who is unclean, and all our righteous acts are like filthy rags (Isaiah 64:6a NIV).

Paying the price for sin, Jesus died and rose again.
But God demonstrates his own love for us in this: While we were still sinners, Christ died for us (Romans 5:8 NIV).

Everyone who trusts in him alone has eternal life.
For God so loved the world that he gave his one and only Son, that whoever believes in him shall not perish but have eternal life (John 3:16 NIV).

Life with Jesus starts now and lasts forever.
I give them eternal life, and they shall never perish; no one will snatch them out of my hand (John 10:28 NIV).

Keep in mind that the GOSPEL acrostic is not designed to be a formula you recite to your friends. Instead, think of it more as a mental map that can serve as general outline when you're explaining the gospel to someone. These six points explain the critical truths someone would need to understand if they wanted to trust in Jesus.

Over the next two devos, we'll flesh out these six core truths of GOSPEL Journey® Message in a little more detail so that you'll be better prepared to have a real conversation with your friends about the gospel.

 # DO SOMETHING!

You've been learning how to open up a spiritual conversation with your friends. But now it's time to learn more about what to say once you've got the God-talk going. Sharing your faith isn't just about swapping stories and opinions; it's about sharing the ultimate story—the gospel, the story of God's interactions with humanity across history.

Take a few minutes to write out the six lines of the GOSPEL acrostic on a small card or paper. Then put it in your backpack or your wallet or somewhere that you will have ready access to it if you need it down the road.

The letter from the GOSPEL acrostic that means the most to me, and why...

DAY 21: GOSPEL JOURNEY[1]

But you should keep a clear mind in every situation. Don't be afraid of suffering for the Lord. Work at telling others the Good News, and fully carry out the ministry God has given you (2 Timothy 4:5).

 ## THE BIG IDEA

Mastering the basics of how to explain the gospel takes some effort, but learning the GOSPEL Journey® Message will help you share Jesus' message in a clear and compelling way.

 ## LISTEN IN

"Because I had the GOSPEL outline to help keep me on track while sharing...I was able to share with a friend, in a coherent way, what God has done for her...things I've always known but rarely felt confident enough to share." —**Anna**

GO DEEPER

To review, the first three stops on the GOSPEL Journey are:

God created us to be with him.

Our sins separate us from God.

Sins cannot be removed by good deeds.

These three simple truths begin the story of God and human interaction. They contain both good and bad news for us. The good news is that we were created to be with God (see Psalm 100:3). The Bible tells us that we were created in God's image and that God loves us. And amazingly, God longs to have a deep and personal relationship with every person ever made!

The bad news is that we've messed up that longed-for relationship. You see, God gave humans free will—the ability to choose good and love God, or to choose evil and turn away from God. We call that evil "sin," and we see the evidence of sin having entered the human scene both in the evil we see around us (murder, hatred, war, injustice) and in the evil we see inside us (selfishness, lust, jealousy, cheating).

Sin entered into our world and tainted our relationship with a holy, just, and perfect God. Our sins separate us from God (see Romans 3:23).

The Bible tells us that there's nothing we can do to erase our sin or remove it in God's eyes. Many people think they can earn their way to heaven by doing good deeds, but the Bible is clear that we can never be good enough to make it into a perfect heaven. James 2:10 says, *For the person who keeps all of the laws except one is as guilty as a person who has broken all of God's laws.* Our holy and perfect God doesn't grade on the curve or give us extra credit for our human efforts to earn our way back into right standing. Sins cannot be removed by good deeds (see Isaiah 64:6). God's just and holy character demands a payment for sin that is greater than anything we could ever pay in and of ourselves.

But don't despair—good news is on the way. God didn't leave us all alone in this mess we made. To be continued...

 # DO SOMETHING!

Write out the first three truths of the GOSPEL in your own words to cement these truths in your mind and heart. Then take a couple of minutes and work on memorizing the G, O, and S lines of the acrostic.

God created us to be with him.

Our sins separate us from God.

Sins cannot be removed by good deeds.

DAY 22: GOSPEL JOURNEY[2]

But God demonstrates his own love for us in this: While we were still sinners, Christ died for us (Romans 5:8 NIV).

 ## THE BIG IDEA

The GOSPEL Journey® Message acrostic can serve as a map when you're sharing your faith with others.

 ## LISTEN IN

"I decided I wanted to tell my friend Josh about Jesus. I knew he was kind of shy, and he can feel a little crowded if you just come right out talking to him about Jesus. So I started slow. I asked him if he were to die tomorrow, where he thought he'd go. He said he had no idea, and I told him that I knew how he could get into heaven, and he wanted to know. I went through the GOSPEL Journey® with him and asked him if he'd known about that before. He said no, but that it made a lot of sense. Then I said that I was telling him about Jesus because I care about him and because I want him to have a personal relationship with Jesus. I asked him if he'd be willing to put his trust in Jesus to forgive his sins so that he could have eternal life, and he said yes!" —**Christina**

GO DEEPER

To review, the final three stops on the GOSPEL Journey are:

Paying the price for sin, Jesus died and rose again.

Everyone who trusts in him alone has eternal life.

Life with Jesus starts now and lasts forever.

Yesterday we looked at the good news/bad news of the first part of the GOSPEL Journey® Message. If you remember, we left off with the bad news of the O and the S lines—that our sins have messed up our relationship with God and there's nothing we can do to make things right again.

But today we're exploring the good news contained in the final three truths of the acrostic. This good news is really good news—in fact, it's the best news on the planet!

The Bible tells us that God loved us so much that he made a way for our relationship to be restored. God did that by sending his Son, Jesus, to die on the cross in our place. Jesus was fully God and fully man. He lived a perfect life, died a horrible death, and rose from the dead for one reason: to redeem us. Jesus paid the price for our sin (see Romans 5:8).

Jesus was the perfect sacrificial payment for the sins of humanity. He paid the price required by the just and holy character God for the forgiveness of our sins. Because of his sacrifice, we can be declared "not guilty."

How does that "not guilty" verdict come to pass? When we place our faith and trust in Jesus. Everyone who trusts in him alone has eternal life. One of the most well-known verses in the Bible says it this way: *For God loved the world so much that he gave his one and only Son, so that everyone who believes in him will not perish but have eternal life" (John 3:16).*

What does the word "believe" mean in this verse? Is it a simple intellectual acknowledgment of Jesus' existence as the Son of God? If that were all "believing" means, even Satan would be a "believer" in Jesus (see James 2:19). No, it means more than that. It means "to trust in, depend on, and rely upon completely."

When we trust in Jesus and fully rely on him for eternal life, we receive salvation as a free gift. And that life with Jesus starts now and lasts forever (see John 10:28).

God draws us into a deep, rich, personal relationship with him, both here and now and forever after. God calls us into his love and sends us out to share that love with others. In a nutshell, it's all about loving God and loving others for an eternity that starts the moment we trust in Jesus.

 DO SOMETHING!

Write out the last three truths of the GOSPEL in your own words. Then take a couple minutes and work on memorizing the P, E, and L part of the acrostic.

Paying the price for sin, Jesus died and rose again.

Everyone who trusts in Jesus alone has eternal life.

_____

_____

Life with Jesus starts now and lasts forever.

_____

_____

DAY 23: DUNAMIS: DYNAMITE!

For I am not ashamed of this Good News about Christ. It is the power of God at work, saving everyone who believes—the Jew first and also the Gentile. This Good News tells us how God makes us right in his sight. This is accomplished from start to finish by faith. As the Scriptures say, "It is through faith that a righteous person has life" (Romans 1:16-17).

 ## THE BIG IDEA

There's an amazing spiritual power inherent in the gospel message that speaks to the deepest needs of the human soul.

 ## LISTEN IN

"My friend used to be in a gang, and he said that he used drugs and alcohol and stuff like that because he had this void in his life. And despite everything he did, he just couldn't fill that hole. He stopped doing all that stuff after his friend got shot in the head in a drive-by because of all that stuff. After that he said, "I just need something to fill this hole." And I said, "Well, I have somebody that could help you; his name is Jesus." And I started explaining the GOSPEL to my friend today over the phone and he was saved. It was just miraculous!" —**Caleb**

 **GO DEEPER**

Caleb lays it right out there for us. The power of the gospel is miraculous. It can reach into the deepest, darkest part of a human heart and blast someone from darkness into light in an instant.

Reread the verse at the top of this page. Did you catch that word *power* in the second sentence? In the Greek (the original language of the New Testament) this word for *power* is *dunamis*, from which we get our word *dynamite*. There's a sense in which the gospel is like a grenade that blows open the prison doors and sets people free to live the amazing life God intended for them. And like a grenade, anyone can pull the pin and see the impact—whether it's explained by a famous evangelist like Billy Graham or a shy 13-year-old girl, the gospel has an inherent power that can transform hearts and lives.

 **DO SOMETHING!**

Put the entire GOSPEL together today and practice explaining it to someone you feel safe with—like a Christian friend, a parent, or your youth leader. Role-play the give-and-take of a real conversation that's centered on these six key truths.

My prayer for God's power and boldness...

_____

_____

_____

_____

DAY 24: SOUL APOLOGETICS

Again I say, don't get involved in foolish, ignorant arguments that only start fights. A servant of the Lord must not quarrel but must be kind to everyone, be able to teach, and be patient with difficult people. Gently instruct those who oppose the truth. Perhaps God will change those people's hearts, and they will learn the truth (2 Timothy 2:23-25).

THE BIG IDEA

Spiritual conversation isn't about winning a debate; it's about relying on the Holy Spirit to help you listen to, engage with, and reach people at a deep spiritual level.

 LISTEN IN

"God just wants us to meet people where they are, remembering that they are his creation. The GOSPEL has given me the ability to do just that by helping me keep my thoughts organized when sharing Christ and allowing me to really listen to people's thoughts instead of worrying about what to say next. Listening is so important when sharing Christ because they see that you care more about them and their destiny than flying through a checklist to heaven." —**Travis**

GO DEEPER

Meeting people on their terrain begins by better understanding where they are. You do that by asking probing questions and listening carefully. I call this approach to understanding where someone is coming from spiritually "soul apologetics."

Traditional apologetics rely on logic and reason to explain things like why we believe in our Creator or why we believe in the Resurrection—and those are legitimate discussion points. But I've learned that you can rarely debate someone into belief in Jesus. Because it's not just people's minds that need to be convinced of the truth of the gospel, it's their souls as well.

While traditional apologetics are often useful when it comes to sharing your faith, they only work effectively if you are in an actual conversation with someone else. If you are genuinely loving and listening to someone, that person's defenses will come down and you can begin to have a real conversation. Think of soul apologetics as a way to ease open the door to a person's soul instead of trying to kick it down with your stacks of facts.

Over and over again in the Gospels, we see Jesus drawing people in by asking them questions that probed deeper and triggered open, honest spiritual discussion.

- In Matthew 16, Jesus asked Peter, "Who do you say that I am?"

- In Mark 10, Jesus asked the rich young ruler, "Why do you call me good?"

- In Luke 20, Jesus asked the religious leaders of his day why they believed what they believed about who the Messiah would be.

Like Jesus, you, too, can ask some probing, open-ended questions that will keep the spiritual dialogue going with your friends. Here are a few examples:

- Have you ever been to a church? How did you feel about your experience there? How did it impact your view of Christians?

- Why do you hold the views of God that you do now? How have your views changed over the years?

- What do you think about Jesus? Do you think he was the Son of God, a good teacher, or something else? What if you're wrong?

- Why do you think there is so much suffering in the world? Why would God allow it? Do you think God cares about humanity? about you?

 DO SOMETHING!

Pray! Pick one of the above questions or come up with one of your own and try it out with a friend today who needs Jesus. Feel free to expand your horizons beyond the original three friends you identified earlier as people you want to reach out to with the good news of Jesus.

Come back at the end of the day and jot down some of your observations about what worked and what you'd try differently next time.

Things I learned about soul apologetics today...

DAY 25: DEALING WITH "CHRISTIAN" BAGGAGE

Jesus spoke to the people once more and said, "I am the light of the world. If you follow me, you won't have to walk in darkness, because you will have the light that leads to life" (John 8:12).

 THE BIG IDEA

For some people, the word *Christian* comes with a lot of baggage. Be sensitive to this issue, and focus on Jesus so you can help friends get past all the labels and stereotypes that sometimes come with the word *Christian*.

LISTEN IN

"My friend had all these oppositions and all these questions, and she had a lot of things holding her back from coming to know who God really is. Unfortunately a lot of the reasons were because of how she's seen a lot of Christians act. I told her to just disconnect all that and disconnect that from God, and I told her that I wanted her just to see God for who he is. I told her some of things he's done for me, and how he's gotten me through trials in my life and the love and the comfort and everything he's brought to me. I looked at her and said, "You know what? The cool thing is that when it's time, it's not me that's going to save you; it's the Holy Spirit. And you'll know that you know that."...And the Holy Spirit got her!

...It kinda got me thinking. I've been her friend for over a year and half now; why couldn't that have happened sooner? It's something that she wanted and something that she needed. It's something that we all need. Why have I kept my mouth quiet for so long? ...I want my friends to know that it's available, and it's life-changing! Now I have a new perspective. I've been so selfish with my faith—it's something that needs to be shared with everybody!" —**Michelle**

 ## GO DEEPER

For some people, the word *Christian* comes with a lot of baggage. Maybe they've been hurt in the past by a shallow, uncaring Christian's words or actions. Maybe they've brushed up against judgmental or hypocritical Christians who soured their view of Christianity. Maybe they've bought the negative stereotype often presented by entertainment media. While many teenagers may have a negative view of Christians, they generally have a positive view of Jesus. So the door's already cracked open!

Try taking a cue from Michelle when you talk to your friends about Jesus, and make sure they understand that you're not trying to recruit them to a membership in the "Christian" club. This is about becoming a follower of Jesus, not about signing up for the baggage-laden labels they may be rebelling against.

 ## DO SOMETHING!

Conduct an informal survey today. You can do this on Facebook® or in person. Ask several people to respond to the two questions below. Watch for opportunities to talk to people further about Jesus.

1.On a scale of 1 to 10, 1 being negative and 10 being positive, how would you rate your response to the word *Christian*?

2.On a scale of 1 to 10, 1 being negative and 10 being positive, how would you rate your response to the name *Jesus*?

Come back and journal about what happened.

What I learned from my Christian/Jesus info-gathering experience...

_____

_____

_____

_____

_____

_____

_____

_____

_____

_____

DAY 26: RELATIONAL AND RELENTLESS EVANGELISM

Yes, I try to find common ground with everyone, doing everything I can to save some. I do everything to spread the Good News and share in its blessings (1 Corinthians 9:22-23).

THE BIG IDEA

Work to find the balance between relationally and relentlessly sharing your faith with your friends.

 LISTEN IN

"Now that I know how important it is to tell people about Jesus, I'm just going to try my hardest every day to keep sharing the gospel with people. I don't care if it's uncool, even though rejection is one my biggest fears. My goal is to keep on going with sharing Jesus and never stop." —**Allie**

GO DEEPER

Relational evangelism focuses on sharing the good news with a loving, listening patience across your network of relationships: friends, classmates, teammates, co-workers, family, neighbors, and so on. These people already know you care about them, and it's only natural that you want to share something as important as the message of Jesus with them.

But relational evangelism can become ineffective and downright wimpy if it slides into a wait-and-see or whatever attitude. That's why it needs to be balanced with a relentless determination to reach your friends by actively pursuing conversations and gently persuading them to consider Christ. Otherwise it becomes all too easy to sit back and simply let your friends observe your life as you wait for them to approach you and ask you questions about Jesus.

So strive for a balance. Relational evangelism loves, listens, and is patient, while relentless evangelism confronts, speaks, and is persistent. It's sort of like a teeter-totter; sometimes one side's up while the other is down, but both are important.

 **DO SOMETHING!**

Ask God to help you find the relational and relentless balance that's right for you as you launch into another spiritual conversation today with a friend who doesn't know Jesus.

Try one of these conversation starters, or come up with your own:

- How have your parents' spiritual beliefs influenced you? Do you believe just like them or do you have a different perspective? (Listen, and then share your own experience.)

- Do you ever feel like God is at work in the midst of a big decision you need to make: classes for next semester, college decisions, relationship choices, whatever? (Listen, and then share about your experience of God being at work in your life.)

- Have you ever felt especially close to God? (Listen, and then share from your experience a time you felt particularly close to God and saw God at work.)

Things I learned today about seeking relational and relentless balance...

_____

_____

_____

_____

_____

_____

_____

_____

_____

DAY 27: KABOOM!

When I first came to you, dear brothers and sisters, I didn't use lofty words and impressive wisdom to tell you God's secret plan. For I decided that while I was with you I would forget everything except Jesus Christ, the one who was crucified. I came to you in weakness—timid and trembling. And my message and my preaching were very plain. Rather than using clever and persuasive speeches, I relied only on the power of the Holy Spirit. I did this so you would trust not in human wisdom but in the power of God (1 Corinthians 2:1-5).

THE BIG IDEA

The power of the Holy Spirit in you and the power of the gospel through you can transform lives forever.

 LISTEN IN

"At the Dare 2 Share evangelism training conference, we were challenged to get out our phones and call the person who was on our mind. So I called my best friend; however, I got her voice message...when I talked to her the next day I used everything I learned about the GOSPEL to lead my best friend to Jesus Christ... and it is the BEST feeling in the whole world to lead someone to God." —**Jess**

GO DEEPER

When you step out in obedience to Jesus' call to live for THE Cause and "go and make disciples," you don't need fancy words or polished debating skills. What you do need is the power of the Holy Spirit working in you and through you. It's the Spirit of God who will fill you with love, compassion, and patience as you reach out to others. God's Spirit will provide the kindness and gentleness you'll need to meet people where they are. God's Spirit will give you the wisdom and insight you'll need to treat each person uniquely and individually.

As you've begun sharing the gospel relationally and relentlessly, maybe you've been wondering how to actually bring someone to a point of decision about trusting in Jesus. Here are two questions you might find helpful after you've explained the GOSPEL to someone:

- Did what I just explained make sense? (If not, go over it again.)

- Is there anything keeping you from putting your faith and trust in Jesus right now?

Of course, it's important not to be pushy, so you must be sensitive about your timing in using these questions. But in my experience, when someone finally understands the message of the gospel, sometimes they need a simple invitation to take that final step of trusting in Jesus.

Keep in mind, too, that oftentimes sharing Jesus with others is a journey. No doubt over these past few weeks you've already learned that you won't necessarily see immediate results at the end of every spiritual conversation you initiate. But regardless of the initial response you get when talking about Jesus, know that God can use you to ignite a spark of curiosity in others that may be fanned into flame at some point in the near or distant future.

DO SOMETHING!

Pray for an opportunity to share the gospel today. Start by initiating a spiritual conversation using some of your opening questions. Then listen, meet them where they are, and share from your heart.

And don't forget, while the GOSPEL acrostic you've learned in the pages of the book is a useful tool for helping you share your faith, if you experience a brain freeze when you're talking to a friend, just remember the message of the cross—God loves us, we're sinners, Christ died for us.

What I have learned so far about sharing my faith...

DAY 28: UNLEASHED FOR THE CAUSE

Again he [Jesus] said, "Peace be with you. As the Father has sent me, so I am sending you" (John 20:21).

 ## THE BIG IDEA

The Father sent Jesus, and Jesus is sending you! So live for his Cause—THE Cause—and share his message with others.

 ## LISTEN IN

"I'm more passionate in my faith now that I'm living THE Cause, stronger and encouraged. God is working in me, changing my heart, helping me to be courageous in the face of adversity. I'm proud to be uncool, unafraid, unashamed. I personally have a lot of friends who have not made a decision for Christ yet, and THE Cause has given me a new motive and a new way to approach them differently and encourage them to make a decision for Christ." —**Jen**

 ## GO DEEPER

Our God is a sending God—2,000 years ago the Father sent Jesus to be the Savior of the world. But God didn't wave a magic wand or snap his fingers and make everyone fall into line and follow him. God gave people a choice then and gives people a choice now. The amazing thing is that God is using you and me to spread the word about this choice and about the free gift of grace, forgiveness, and salvation. In all his wisdom and power, God has chosen to use us, his followers, as his representatives.

Paul puts it this way in 2 Corinthians 5:18-20:

And all of this is a gift from God, who brought us back to himself through Christ. And God has given us this task of reconciling people to him. For God was in Christ, reconciling the world to himself, no longer counting people's sins against them. And he gave us this wonderful message of reconciliation. So we are Christ's ambassadors; God is making his appeal through us. We speak for Christ when we plead, "Come back to God!"

Did you catch that? We are Christ's ambassadors; God is making his appeal through us. What an incredible privilege and responsibility—to speak for Christ and plead with our friends to *"Come back to God!"*

As the Father sent Jesus, now Jesus is sending you.

 # DO SOMETHING!

There's no getting around it: Jesus is sending you out on a big job. Sharing your faith is the most important thing you'll ever do in life because all eternity hangs in the balance. Spend some time writing a quick note to God about how you're feeling about your job description, and then step out and initiate a spiritual conversation with someone today.

How I'm feeling about being Jesus' ambassador to my friends...

_____

_____

_____

_____

_____

_____

_____

_____

_____

_____

DAY 29: DISCIPLE CYCLES

But some of them became obstinate; they refused to believe and publicly maligned the Way. So Paul left them. He took the disciples with him and had discussions daily in the lecture hall of Tyrannus. This went on for two years, so that all the Jews and Greeks who lived in the province of Asia heard the word of the Lord (Acts 19:9-10 NIV).

 ## THE BIG IDEA

Jesus is calling you to make disciples who, in turn, make disciples so that the message of the gospel can be multiplied in life after life.

 ## LISTEN IN

"From the moment when I finally saw the truth, I wanted to tell everyone! My friends, family, people on the bus and at the grocery store were all at risk of being "gospelized." The first thing I did was to make a list of people I wanted to share the gospel with, and number one on that list was my best friend. She was one of the first people I told of my life-changing experience, and that first conversation led to another, which led to yet another. It wasn't long before she put her faith and trust in Jesus. After that she jumped on board the same faith-sharing journey I am on and began telling everyone about Jesus, even her ex-boyfriend! He came to church with us one week, and though he isn't ready yet...he is on both of our lists." —**Vanessa**

 ## GO DEEPER

In the book of Acts we see Jesus' message spreading like wildfire. As new believers trusted in Jesus and became Christians, they, in turn, took the message to their friends, who shared it with their friends. The message went viral, spreading in ever-widening circles of relationship until the transforming power of the gospel eventually reached every corner of the earth.

As you share the gospel and bring others to a point of trusting in Jesus, it's important to understand that your job doesn't end there! New followers of Christ need to grow in their faith.

It's important to get them connected to a church body or youth group. They also need to be encouraged to share the good news they've discovered with their own friends who need Jesus. Their excitement and enthusiasm as a result of God's work in their hearts should bubble over into sharing this most amazing message with others. But in case they have some evangephobia of their own, you need to be there to give them some encouragement and guidance.

 ## DO SOMETHING!

Consider some of the following approaches for getting serious about making disciples who make disciples. Choose one and get started today. Or come up with your own idea.

- Invite someone to youth group.

- Recruit some friends and make plans to go through the key principles found in this devotional.

- Pray together over the phone and hold each other accountable about initiating spiritual conversations with others.

- Help a new Christian learn how to share the GOSPEL Journey® Message with friends.

- Sign yourself and your friends up to receive the free weekly devotional resource "Soul Fuel" by going to dare2share.org.

- Start a one-on-one Bible study with a new Christian to help them grow in their walk with God. For help with this, download a copy of Dare 2 Share's discipleship resource "Now Grow!" at dare2share.org/store

My prayer and plan for encouraging new Christians to grow and share their faith...

DAY 30: CALL ME! IT'S URGENT!

And this is what God has testified: He has given us eternal life, and this life is in his Son. Whoever has the Son has life; whoever does not have God's Son does not have life. I have written this to you who believe in the name of the Son of God, so that you may know you have eternal life (1 John 5:11-13).

 ## THE BIG IDEA

You never know when your chance to talk to others about the gospel might slip away forever. So be focused and purposeful as you go make disciples. It's urgent!

 ## LISTEN IN

"I'm starting on a new challenge and any of you can join me, but I'm writing down the names of 100 people I know that don't believe in Christ, or that I don't know if they believe and I'm going to talk to every one of them. Then I'm writing down 100 names of people I know who are Christians, and I'm going to tell them about the urgency of talking to their friends about Jesus. Well, enough talk, it's time to start!" —**Jimmy**

 ## GO DEEPER

Jimmy's goal is big! Maybe you aren't ready to tackle a list of 100. Maybe God is calling you to begin with three or four friends who need Jesus and to challenge a handful of Christian friends to get involved with THE Cause alongside you.

No matter how many friends you have on your radar, it's important to bring urgency to your efforts. Your window of opportunity for reaching your school friends gets smaller with every passing day. Even though graduation might feel like it's a million miles away, every day it gets closer. And you never know when life might get turned totally upside down by a move, car accident, suicide, or serious illness.

Besides, why would you want your friends to go even another day apart from the good stuff Jesus bring to our lives: love, forgiveness, purpose, and transforming power? So make the most of your opportunities to share Jesus, and get serious about recruiting others to join you in this great endeavor. Make it a team effort. Encourage each other along the way. You can also connect with thousands of other teenagers who are committed to living THE Cause by going to facebook.com/livethecause.com.

 DO SOMETHING!

Revisit your list of friends you want to reach for Jesus. Pray for them and have at least one spiritual conversation today with one of them.

My friends who need Jesus...

1.

2.

3.

4.

5.

Then think and pray about which Christian friends you might be able to recruit to join you in living out THE Cause of Christ. Talk to at least one of them today about joining you on this adventure.

My Christian friends who could help live THE Cause...

1.

2.

3.

4.

5.

Pray! Face down your fears. Fuel up your **EVANGELISM** passion. Tap into the power of God's Spirit. Bring God up with your friends who need Jesus. Share your faith story and Jesus' gospel story. And get your Christian friends to join you in living out THE Cause of Christ. Together you can reach your generation for Christ and change your world!

My letter to God asking him to help me every step of the way on this evangelism adventure...

_____

_____

_____

_____

More books from Dare 2 Share

30-day Student Devotional

Reach Out...Don't Freak Out will motivate and mobilize you to reach your friends for Christ. Loaded with practical tips and conversation starters, *Reach Out* will help you discover your own unique sharing style and equip you to reach out without freaking out!

Jared is an atheist with an attitude.

Kailey is a new believer with a temper.

Follow the story of their senior year and find out what can happen when just one teen is passionate about the mission of Jesus to reach the lost.

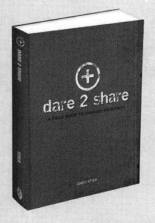

Share your faith with anyone, anytime, anywhere!

Dare 2 Share: A Field Guide serves as a ready reference for relationally sharing your faith. Throw it in your backpack for easy access to the invaluable faith-sharing tips and tools you'll find in this practical, real world resource. Features profiles on various belief systems, including compliments and conversation starters that will help you open up honest, authentic spiritual dialogue.

Available at www.Dare2Share.org

Share your faith with your friends using the latest music, movies, TV and trends

soul fuel
making disciples who make disciples

Soul Fuel is a FREE weekly online resource designed to help you keep THE Cause front and center in your life. Get practical insights and ideas for relationally and relentlessly sharing your faith!

Free Soul Fuel Discussion Guides are also available for youth leaders.

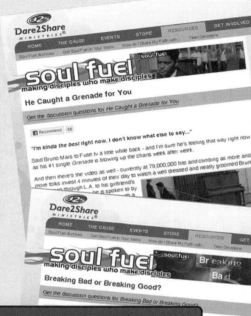

Sign up to recieve soul fuel in your inbox at
dare2share.org/soulfuel

 Or check out Soul Fuel each week on
facebook/livethecause